EAT LIKE A LOCAL-CONNECTICUT

Connecticut Food Guide

Angelina Rosa Truax

D1444510

CZYK Publishing Since 2011.

Eat Like a Local

Lock Haven, PA

ISBN: 9798662608368

BOOK DESCRIPTION

Are you excited about planning your next trip?
Do you want an edible experience? Would you
like some culinary guidance from a local? If you
answered yes to any of these questions, then this Eat
Like a Local book is for you. Eat Like a Local -
Connecticut by Author Angelina Rosa Truax offers
the inside scoop on food in Connecticut. Culinary
tourism is an important aspect of any travel
experience. Food has the ability to tell you a story of
a destination, its landscapes, and culture on a single
plate. Most food guides tell you how to eat like a
tourist. Although there is nothing wrong with that, as
part of the Eat Like a Local series, this book will give
you a food guide from someone who has lived at your
next culinary destination.

In these pages, you will discover advice on having
a unique edible experience. This book will not tell
you exact addresses or hours but instead will give you
excitement and knowledge of food and drinks from a
local that you may not find in other travel food
guides.

Eat like a local. Slow down, stay in one place, and get to know the food, people, and culture. By the time you finish this book, you will be eager and prepared to travel to your next culinary destination.

OUR STORY

Traveling has always been a passion of the creator of the Eat Like a Local book series. During Lisa's travels in Malta, instead of tasting what the city offered, she ate at a large fast-food chain. However, she realized that her traveling experience would have been more fulfilling if she had experienced the best of local cuisines. Most would agree that food is one of the most important aspects of a culture. Through her travels, Lisa learned how much locals had to share with tourists, especially about food. Lisa created the Eat Like a Local book series to help connect people with locals which she discovered is a topic that locals are very passionate about sharing. So please join me and: Eat, drink, and explore like a local.

TABLE OF CONTENTS

18. Lunch
19. Best Cocktail
20. Best Spirit
21. Best Beer For Beer Enthusiasts
22. Pour Another Glass Of Wine
23. Best Burger
24. Best Bread
25. Best Barbeque
26. Best Steakhouse
27. Best Diner
28. Best Late-Night Dining
29. Best Grinder
30. Best Hot Dog
31. Best Indian
32. Best Italian
33. Best Farmers Market
34. Best Lobster Roll
35. Best New England Clam Chowder
36. Best Pie
37. Best Pizza
38. Best Pub Food
39. Best Sushi
40. Tacos & Tequila
41. Best Thai
42. Best Wings
43. Sweet Tooth

DEDICATION

I dedicate this book in honor of my late father, Joseph. He was my protector, best friend, and biggest cheerleader. I would prefer it if you were here to share in the realization of my dream. Instead, to celebrate, I will drink a Coca Cola and eat gummy bears like we did together when I was a child.

ABOUT THE AUTHOR

Angelina was born and raised in Connecticut. A foodie at heart, her hobbies include watching movies, going to see musicals, and traveling. Her poetry was included in the anthologies Learning To Fly and The Best Poems And Poets Of 2002. In 2004 she penned a book of poetry titled Poem For My Father. You can read her unique view on feature films on the mxdwn Movies website, where she is a feature writer. She enjoys writing different genres and pushing herself to the next level creatively. She currently resides in the northwest hills of Connecticut with her husband, son, and dog.

As an Italian-American, food has been a significant part of her life. Angelina's paternal grandmother, Jean, wasn't much of a chef but stressed the importance of family coming together for a meal. Angelina's childhood was spent bonding with her extended family with food never in short supply. Jean and Angelina had a special connection, exchanging letters when they weren't together. She learned the secret of making lasagna in Jean's kitchen and now makes it for her family.

On her mother's side, she watched her maternal grandmother, Maria, cook food with ease. The kitchen was an extension of herself, never measuring or seeking the guidance of a recipe. She relied on the smell and taste of the food rather than what was on a sheet of paper. Angelina would spend part of her summer with Maria as a child watching her cook with love as the secret ingredient. Before her passing, Maria gifted Angelina the recipe for doughnuts and a rolling pin to continue the tradition of home-made doughnuts.

HOW TO USE THIS BOOK

The goal of this book is to help culinary travelers either dream or experience different edible experiences by providing opinions from a local. The author has made suggestions based on their own knowledge. Please do your own research before traveling to the area in case the suggested locations are unavailable.

Travel Advisories: As a first step in planning any trip abroad, check the Travel Advisories for your intended destination.
https://travel.state.gov/content/travel/en/traveladvisories/traveladvisories.html

FROM THE PUBLISHER

Traveling can be one of the most important parts of a person's life. The anticipation and memories that you have are some of the best. As a publisher of the *Eat Like a Local*, Greater Than a Tourist, as well as the popular *50 Things to Know* book series, we strive to help you learn about new places, spark your imagination, and inspire you. Wherever you are and whatever you do I wish you safe, fun, and inspiring travel.

Lisa Rusczyk Ed. D.
CZYK Publishing

*"The secret of success in life is
to eat what you like and let the food
fight it out inside."*

– Mark Twain

Welcome to Connecticut! Connecticut gets a poor reputation from people inside and outside the state. In the movies, Connecticut is usually portrayed as this wealthy state full of country clubs and sweater vests where celebrities go on vacation or retire. In reality, Connecticut is a quaint state bursting with history and humble living.

Situated evenly between New York City and Boston, Connecticut is often looked over for tourism. Big city adventures are enjoyable, but if you want some R&R, Connecticut is perfect for a quick getaway.

Tourists and most residents take the state for granted. There are many hidden gems tucked away in the nutmeg state to explore. The best part is, with a diversity of cultures coming together, there is a wide variety of food to try. I like driving to a nearby town and choosing a place to eat at random, with a group of people waiting to go inside. The building doesn't have to look fancy for the food to be good. The best dishes can be served from a hole in the wall! I've included different kinds of food from various cultures that will become your new favorites.

I have set out to change the conversation around my state regarding food and fun. I have nothing against national chain stores or restaurants. Much of their menu can be good to great, but as your guide, I have laid out for you the best places to eat and explore that can only be found in Connecticut. I set out to write this as a love letter to the local foods and activities that have shaped me during my lifetime here. I hope by the end of this book, you will want to come to my state to try one of my highlighted gems.

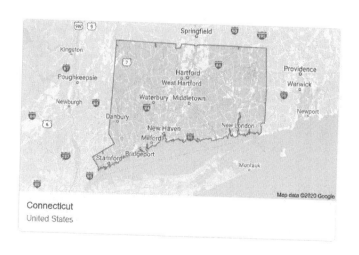

Connecticut
United States

Hartford
Connecticut
Climate

	High	Low
January	36	18
February	39	21
March	48	29
April	60	39
May	71	49
June	79	58
July	84	64
August	83	63
September	75	54
October	63	42
November	52	34
December	41	24

GreaterThanaTourist.com

Temperatures are in Fahrenheit degrees.
Source: NOAA

1. WHY VISIT

"Life begins at the end of your comfort zone."

– Neale Donald Walsch

If you're checking us out on a globe, Connecticut is that minuscule bumpy land between New York City and Boston. You can fit the greater Houston, Texas area on top of the entire state! Connecticut is home to Yale University, Coast Guard Academy, and the home of Mark Twain. If you are anywhere in New England, Connecticut is an easy day-trip or weekend getaway. While visiting, it is easy to get to and from the state. The best, and only way, to get around is by car. Year-round something is going on, and there is something to see. The scenery is gorgeous, no matter the time of year. I've had people come to visit me to see the leaves change or to see snow for the first time.

Your trip can easily be broken down into themes. You can unravel the history of the United States, visit famous places, and even take in award-winning theatre. All can be done by channeling your inner foodie, trying one or all of the unique eateries in the state.

2. HOW CONNECTICUT HAS SHAPED ME

"Travel makes one modest; you see what tiny place you occupy in the world."

– Gustave Flaubert

Living in Connecticut has given me many privileges concerning immersive learning. In junior high, I took home economics, which I owe to learning how to sew a button, make a pillow, and how to make an apple pie. In elementary school, we took a field trip to our town's historical museum. I remember walking hand-in-hand from the school to the museum center. I didn't realize it at the time, but it was that field trip that sparked my love of history and learning. At the Canton Historical Museum, I learned about the history of my city, and it's contributions to manufacturing. Back then, I was more interested in the penny candy they sold unaware of the seed that was being planted.

We even visited outer state places, like New York City and Boston, to add to what was being taught. In eighth grade, we loaded onto a bus and drove the six-hour plus voyage to Washington, D.C. Instead of sleeping through history lessons in a classroom, we got to dig deep with interactive learning by seeing all the monuments and soaking in information from all the museums the cities had to offer.

Each city had a field trip with excellent storytellers as guides. Seeing them retell history, so lively as they spoke, has taught me more than sitting at the same table with my nose between some pages. I owe those experiences to my town and my state. From what I have heard from people from other parts of the country, this type of learning was not universal. As budgets per student have dropped, the costs of field trips are sacrificed to provide primary education for growing classrooms. In turn, students don't get to have the same experiences I had in school. I feel fortunate for being exposed to a "see and touch" style of education, and I will always be grateful.

3. LEARN SOME NEW PHRASES

"I'm from Connecticut, and we don't have any dialects. Well, I don't think we have any dialects, and yeah, it's very complex. That Rhode Island/Massachusetts, New England region, is arguably the hardest dialect to nail."

– Seth MacFarlane

In Connecticut, we can drop consonants in the middle of words while using unusual terms or phrases in such a way that leaves you scratching your head.

Connecticut is unofficially the nutmeg state. You will see nutmeg being advertised in baked goods with a cutesy name. We like nutmeg so much that you will hear someone referring to themselves as a "Nutmegger."

When asking for recommendations on where to visit, you may hear someone suggest Mystic. Mystic can refer to the town, aquarium, or seaport.

If someone is giving you directions and tells you the Merritt is the only way to get there, they are referring to the Merritt Parkway. Be warned drivers tend to be aggressive, especially during rush hour.

Speaking of driving and directions, if someone tells you where you're going is located on the pike, they are referring to the Berlin Turnpike. The pike has many u-ey's, which we call a u-turn.

While visiting, if you want to buy some liquor, you need to ask where the nearest packie, or package store, is.

We do not have garage sales; we have tag sales.

There are many names for sandwiches such as a sub, hoagie, po'boy, zep, or hero. In Connecticut, we call them grinders.

Uconn is short for the University of Connecticut, and the mascot for the university is the husky dog. Uconn pride runs deep. Due to the university's partnership with the local government, Uconn is at the core of the state's medical programs. The locals and the state government have adopted the mascot to refer to individual clinics, individual hospitals, or the entire hospital system as well as the food stamp program, and the state Medicaid.

Only in Connecticut would this bit of advice make sense, "You probably want to go to the Husky to get that looked at, and while you're there, you can see if you qualify for Husky. If you qualify, you may need to call Husky and see if there's other Husky you can get like Husky food or Husky rides to the doctor."

4. BEST TIME TO VISIT

The people who venture up north to see the leaves are commonly referred to as leafers. Who could blame them? The best time to visit Connecticut is also my favorite time of year, autumn. Seeing red, orange, or yellow leaves in a picture doesn't come close to the real thing. With the fall comes hot apple cider paired with a warm apple cider doughnut. There is apple picking, corn mazes, and pumpkin patches.

I can see the Farmington river from the back of my house. I enjoy sitting on my deck and drinking a glass of wine, looking at the foliage. The crisp air with the array of colors makes Connecticut heaven on earth during the fall.

5. AMOUNT OF TIME NEEDED

Connecticut may be a small state, but because it is compact, you don't need to book out a large chunk of time to visit. It takes less than two hours to drive through in any direction. Even if you only have a weekend, that is plenty of time to soak in sites. In just a few days, you can hike, sail, or go back in time.

6. WHERE TO STAY: B&B

One of my favorite places to visit is Old Wethersfield. Old Wethersfield is the largest historic district in Connecticut and has a low-key vibe, great food, and things to see. Being centrally located for easy access to surrounding towns, I would suggest staying at the Silas W Robbins House Bed & Breakfast. The B&B has many restaurants and attractions within walking distance. Head down to the cove, grab a slice at Village Pizza, or old fashion candy at Old Wethersfield Country Store. The gorgeous structure of the Silas W Robbins House you see today wouldn't be possible without the restoration of 2001 – 2007 by Shireen and John Aforismo.

7. WHERE TO STAY: HISTORIC VIBE

Connecticut is a historical state, so there are many places to stay that are rich with history. Some buildings have plaques detailing related bits for everyone to see. Simsbury is home to the Pinchot Sycamore, the biggest tree in Connecticut. Simsbury has been in establishment since the 1600s and ranked in the top 10 best placed to live. I'm not surprised it ranked that high with everything the town has. There are miles of trails to hike, bike, or bird watch. The town offers access to the river for kayaking or fishing. There are golf courses and a world-renowned ice skating rink. I would suggest saying at the Simsbury 1820 House. Your room will either be located in the main house or the home's original Carriage House.

8. WHERE TO STAY: ULTIMATE PRIVACY

For a quiet, relaxing stay, my suggestion is Abbey's Lantern Hill Inn. The inn is perfect because you get to experience nature and peace. You can explore nearby beaches then wind down undisturbed. If you change your mind and want to have an adventure, you can walk to Foxwoods Casino. You can also hop in your car for a 10-minute drive to Mohegan Sun Casino and Mystic. Even if you're not into the gambling scene, there are mall sized areas full of Native American decor, shopping centers, food options, and entertainment venues to visit.

9. UNIQUE PLACES TO SHOP

Malls and shopping centers are a dime a dozen in America. Everywhere you travel, they have the same stores in similar malls. If you want to bring back a unique gift that cannot be duplicated anywhere else, I would suggest shopping off the beaten path.

Atticus Bookstore Café in New Haven brings my two loves together, reading and food. The selection of books in a small space is impressive, and the café brings an element of class. Top off a book selection with a cup of coffee, and you'll never want to leave.

Cindy's Unique Shop is a thrift and consignment shop in Wallingford, specializing in hidden treasures.

The owner is the sweetest person, and I've come out with one of a kind items.

For fellow bibliophiles, The Book Barn in Niantic is my go-to. The Book Barn in this town has three locations, which are the Main Barn, Downtown, and Chapter Three. Not only is the staff kind and helpful, but the funky atmosphere makes book browsing more fun. Even if I go thinking I am just going to look, I always find something I've been looking for and have to get!

For a blast from the not so distant past, head to New England Jukebox and Collectibles in Vernon. They sell soda machines, jukeboxes and parts, and pinball machines, to name a few. I like to go and look at the different neon signs all lit up.

For fellow music lovers, I would recommend Gerosa Records in Brookfield. I prefer listening to music on vinyl, which is why I'm glad places like Gerosa still exist in this world of streaming music. I found different artists that became my favorites at Gerosa. When you go back home, you can still purchase from their library on their eBay and Merch stores.

10. MADE IN CONNECTICUT

Despite it not being a "hidden gem," a visit to Connecticut would not be complete without a visit to the Pez Visitor Center. While at the visitor center, you will be able to see the largest collection of Pez memorabilia, a Pez motorcycle built by Orange County Choppers, and the largest Pez dispenser. At the retail store, you can bring a piece of Pez and Connecticut home with you.

11. FAMOUS PLACES: FOOD EDITION

Tucked away in the village of Mystic is Mystic Pizza. The 1988 movie of the same name was filmed on location in Mystic and surrounding towns. You can eat in the film's pizzeria that Julia Roberts's waited at. In addition to tasting their pizza, I recommend trying their cajun fries and New England clam chowder. After you eat, pick up some merchandise to have a "little slice of heaven" back home.

In New Haven at Louis' Lunch, is the birthplace of the hamburger. Not only is Louis' Lunch recognized by the Library of Congress as the birthplace of the hamburger sandwich, but the eatery was featured on The Travel Channel and The Food Network. Stop by and eat a hamburger and drink a Connecticut made Foxon Park Soda.

12. DOG-FRIENDLY RESTAURANTS

I love going on vacation with my dog, Oliver. Pet-friendly hotels are becoming increasingly popular, and dog-friendly restaurants are starting to see momentum as well. Oliver and I love going to The Elbow Room in West Hartford. Not only is the food delicious, but the outdoor seating in the center of West Hartford is an excellent spot for people-watching. Every time I go there, the waitstaff is friendly, and they make sure to give my dog plenty of head scratches. When you go, make sure to try the lobster mac and cheese or one of their burgers.

Another favorite spot of mine is Pink Basil in Mystic. They have excellent sushi options and the best Pad Thai you've ever tasted. Not only will you be well taken care of, but your best friend will too. Oliver was given the royal treatment; they provided him with a dog bowl with ice in the water and a container of chicken.

13. CASH ONLY WORTH THE TRIP TO THE ATM

There aren't many places that don't accept credit or debit card cards as a payment option. I don't regularly keep cash on me. Like many others, I've been spoiled by the convenience of my debit card. McGrane's On The Green in Winsted is worth the trip to the ATM. When I go to McGrane's for breakfast, I always get the biscuits and gravy. It brings back memories of visiting my aunt in South Carolina; she always makes me biscuits and gravy when I visit her. If I go for lunch or dinner, I almost (definitely) order the Yankee pot roast. Everything is cooked to perfection and is the right meal for cold New England days.

My favorite activity to do in the summer is to take my son to the drive-in movie theatre. The Pleasant

Valley Drive-In in Barkhamsted is one of the last drive-in movie theaters around. I grew up playing with my siblings in front of the big screen before the movie started. Going there brings back great memories, and I'm happy it is still around for my son to experience. To add to the nostalgia of times past, they are cash-only. The admission is low, and they have a carload night on Thursdays where the rate is per car instead of per person. I love getting popcorn and ice cream, and my son gets a burger with fries. If you are coming in the summer, catch a movie under the stars!

14. BEST COFFEE

I am a coffee lover, well, a coffee addict. When I need my coffee fix, I head over to The Coffee Trade in Avon. The Coffee Trade is without an equal to what makes them special. They sell antiques and unique gifts in their shop. The owners are the nicest people and quickly learn your name and favorite coffee. You can buy a cup to go, or you can purchase grounds to make at home. Stop by and order an iced Irish cream coffee, your life will change!

15. BEST BREAKFAST

The best breakfast place hands down is Cosmic Omelet in Manchester. I am not much of an egg person, but when I am in the mood for some crazy good eggs, I head to Cosmic. Right on their menu, it states that they take breakfast seriously, and that is an understatement. Besides making a killer omelet, Cosmic supports local artists by inviting them to exhibit their art inside the restaurant. Since many of the pieces are for sale, the art frequently changes, so I get to see new things each time I go there to eat. It is hard to suggest one thing since everything on the menu is so delicious. However, one of my favorite things to order is Miss Piggy's Junk In The Trunk.

16. WHO NEEDS NYC FOR BAGELS

New York City bagels are delicious. When I can't go to New York for my bagel fix, I head over to one of my favorite places for bagels. Bruegger's Bagels has been a favorite place for many years; they have five locations throughout Connecticut. The location I frequent is in Avon. The bagels are made with only five simple ingredients and are the New York-style that I love. Their cream cheese is made in Vermont and tastes great on everything, including breakfast or lunch sandwiches. A surprisingly popular recommendation is the hot tuna.

Another excellent option for bagels is Brookside Bagels in Simsbury. Besides breakfast sandwiches, they make an incredible BLT, and their homefries are amazing. Finally, over the mountain (Avon Mountain) in West Hartford is Lox Stock & Bagels. They have bagels, many spread options, and wraps. My son loves the buffalo chicken wrap or a bagel with the jalapeno cream cheese.

17. BEST BRUNCH

When I was getting married, my girlfriends brought me to The Water's Edge Resort And Spa in Westbrook for their Sunday brunch. We sat outside and had a gorgeous view of the water while we drank our mimosas. My favorite part had nothing to do with the view or the food. A gentleman was playing the piano, I requested Piano Man, and he played it for me. Then, after a few mimosas, I asked for Free Bird, and he played it for me too! Reservations fill up quickly, be sure to book your Sunday brunch as soon as possible, especially if you plan on going for a holiday like Mother's Day.

18. LUNCH

My favorite spot for lunch is Beau's Burger Shack in Canton. The owner is friendly and makes the best chili in New England. The head cook is fantastic, as well. She remembers what my son orders and makes him feel like a celebrity by knowing what he likes. Everything is good at Beau's. You might need to go multiple times to try all the great stuff they have to offer. My favorites are the chili dog, pulled pork sandwich, and buffalo chicken wrap. Make sure to try a milkshake and the chili cheese waffle fries.

It is really easy to mess up pizza. The crust can be doughy, and the pizza overly greasy. Another great place for lunch is Cozzy's Pizzeria in Kent. The crust is perfect, and the pizza is not greasy. While eating there, I am treated like family, and everything I order is yummy. My favorite thing to get is a slice and a Ceasar salad.

For a sandwich, I like to head to the Better Half Bistro in Pine Meadow. The specials change daily and never disappoint. My son loves their buffalo wrap, and my husband either gets their Italian or Rachel sandwich. They have a small bakery, and I always cross my fingers that they haven't sold out of their cheddar biscuits. I sometimes will go for breakfast, where they make the most delicious breakfast sandwiches. The coffee is excellent, too, with exciting flavors to try!

Another lunch spot to try is the Harvest Café in Simsbury. The café serves breakfast, but I usually stop by for lunch. You can never go wrong ordering a burger, but I recommend the chicken salad croissant. They also have a bakery that sells cakes, cupcakes, and other sweet treats. For the treats, there isn't something I order each time. I let the sweet treats speak to me, and I request that before I go.

19. BEST COCKTAIL

Tisane Euro Asian Café in Hartford is the only option if you are looking for a unique and delicious cocktail. They offer coffee, tea, and Sunday brunch in addition to their dinner options. One of my favorites is the Espresso Martea-ni, which has espresso, vanilla vodka, and nutty chocolate liqueurs in it. My other favorite is The Naughty Girl Scout, per the menu, which is "like a creamy thin mint in a glass with a spanking." I recommend trying the BBQ pork spring rolls, and the buffalo chicken sandwich.

20. BEST SPIRIT

Hickory Ledges Farm in Canton produces and distributes Full Moonshine. Full Moonshine also sells hand sanitizer and various other merchandise. My favorite flavors to drink straight are apple pie and cranberry because they are all delicious. I like to use Pete's Maple "80" and Circa 1797 in my cocktails or on the rocks. You can buy Full Moonshine across Connecticut, at two locations in Manhattan, and online.

21. BEST BEER FOR BEER ENTHUSIASTS

For being such a small state, Connecticut has many breweries. The one that I frequent the most is Brewery Legitimus in New Hartford. Despite it not being as large as other breweries, it offers a taproom, outdoor beer garden, and a rotating schedule of food trucks. The outdoor beer garden is enjoyable because I can bring my dog with me. With Satan's Kingdom recreation area just down the road, I usually order the Satan's Kingdom Belgian Strong Golden Ale or Champlain Orchards Foxboro Rose.

Another great brewery is the Thomas Hooker Brewery in Bloomfield. The brewery is open to tours, private events, and dogs are welcome on the patio outside. What I love about this brewery is that they have a kitchen inside. Few things are more enjoyable in the summer than enjoying a cold beer with pizza, nachos, and more.

Also in Bloomfield is Back East Brewing. This brewery offers tours, contact-free Saturday drive-through, and award-winning beer. I like the clever names of the beers that they offer. Currently, they have the Tony Goes Dancing DIPA, Unicorn Farm

IPA, and Misty Mountain IPA. Later in June 2020, they will be releasing the Ice Cream Man IPA and Double Scoop DIPA. I will be waiting on the release dates to get a can of each to try!

My last brewery recommendation in Connecticut is Two Roads Brewing in Stratford. In addition to their brewery tours, food truck offerings, and events/festivals, they are implementing a retailer relief draft program. Due to the recent hardships that many retailers are facing due to COVID-19, Two Roads is providing deep discounts on their draft beers to Connecticut restaurants. Since the effects of COVID-19 will have a lasting impact, I urge you to check them out so they can continue to assist restaurants get "back on the road."

22. POUR ANOTHER GLASS OF WINE

When most people think about wine, besides France and Italy, most people think of California. Like the beer selection, there are many wineries in Connecticut. The CT Wine Trail is the best way to sample and enjoy the wine across the state. There are currently 24 participating wineries on the CT Wine Trail. It's a tough job sampling all the wine, but someone has to do it, wine as well be you. If the wine trail seems too daunting of a task, you can always go to the summer Connecticut Wine Festival. Coming to the state in the winter? No problem, there is a winter wine trail as well.

23. BEST BURGER

I love a good burger, and not all burgers are created equal. Connecticut is the birthplace of the hamburger, so there are high expectations. Max Burger in West Hartford is my favorite place for a burger. My favorite burgers to get are the Maple Whiskey and Texican. Most of the burgers are 8oz except for the Max Classics and Turkey burgers. Whatever burger you decide to try, I strongly urge you to have the truffle fries or the bacon & brussels sprouts.

24. BEST BREAD

I love bread. Growing up, my favorite snack was bread with butter and a cup of tea. For my bread, I go to Bantam Bread in Bantam. They carry 12 types of bread, but my favorites are the caraway rye, pain de Campagne, and semolina batard. If you aren't in the mood for plain bread, they offer sweets and desserts too. I recommend the angel biscuits! I support Bantam Bread because they feature local products from teas, to jams, and even greeting cards.

25. BEST BARBEQUE

I'm going to confess that I used to hate eating barbeque. I now know the reason was that all that time, I wasn't eating Bear's Smokehouse BBQ. They have five locations around Connecticut, so no matter which part you are visiting, there is most likely a Bear's close-by. They also have a food truck that makes the rounds to breweries and other events. I recently learned they had a brewery in New Haven. I haven't been, but that is my next place to try.

They have 10 (including one meatless) choices of meat. I always order the Mac Attack with pulled pork. The Mac Attack is Mac and Cheese topped with the meat of your choice. My husband likes the Bear Attack, which is cornbread topped with mac & cheese mixed with burnt ends brisket and smothered in BBQ sauce. As a side note, my Texan husband thinks himself as a BBQ/Smokehouse enthusiast, and Bear's is where we go when he's homesick.

If you're in Hartford and have already eaten Bear's and want something different but are craving more Bear's, then there's a surprising solution for this conundrum. Across the street is the Blind Pig Pizza Co. They use the meats from Bear's and offer a menu carrying that Bear's-style boldness and quality in a great pizza joint and watering hole in one establishment.

26. BEST STEAKHOUSE

I mentioned near the beginning that I wouldn't include popular national chains in this book. I didn't want to add a place like Texas Roadhouse, even though the food is generally good, yet they have around 600 locations worldwide and are in 49 states. I do want to break that rule for my steakhouse section because a lot of great steakhouses don't stay mom and pop and almost always grow into a small "chain." When you're near Hartford and feeling the grille experience, I recommend visiting Ted's Montana Grill. There's a definite feel of a classic saloon in the 19th century. The cornerstone of the menu is American Bison, selling more than any restaurant in the world.

It's interesting to note that Ted's Connecticut uses sustainability practices in all aspects of their business. They order small batches throughout the day to reduce the amount of waste, order from local growers as much as possible, and use sustainable choice supplies such as paper straws and Boraxo soap. Yet, the main reason it's on this list is because of the food itself.

Whether you order chicken, chili, Beef or Bison, burgers or steak, well done or rare, the food is always excellent. For steak enthusiasts and my husband, "rare" apparently means slaughtered 15 minutes before it is served. In my husband's words, "Ted's does not disappoint!"

27. BEST DINER

The New Hartford Diner in New Hartford is my favorite place to eat. The staff have felt like a second family for years now. They know my family's usual orders and have my son's school picture hanging up behind the counter. No matter what time of day, the food is delicious. For a while, I would order a French omelet with a blueberry pancake to share with my son. Now that he is older, he eats the entire pancake, and I switched to breakfast sandwiches with home fries. They have daily specials, which I usually order from for lunch or dinner. Unless they have biscuits and gravy as a breakfast special, then I order that.

28. BEST LATE-NIGHT DINING

A downside of living in Connecticut is that restaurants close relatively early compared to other areas. I like the Twin Colony Diner in Torrington because it is open till 2:00 AM Sunday - Thursday and 24 hours on Friday and Saturday. They have an extensive menu with all the diner favorites. I like to get the challah French toast with bacon on the side. When you visit, make sure to leave room for their NY style cheesecake.

29. BEST GRINDER

Grinders are popular because it is a quick meal on the go. Nardelli's has some of the best grinders I have ever had. With 15 locations across the state, I am always close to Nardelli's. The menu is extensive, with a wide variety of cold and hot grinders. Also, they have delicious cannolis if you leave room for dessert. When you pay, make sure to leave a tip. Whenever they get a tip, the cashier rings a bell, and every staff member shouts, "Grazie."

30. BEST HOT DOG

I like my hot dogs with nacho cheese, onions, and chili. When I am home making my own hot dog with chili, I use Mucke's hot dogs. If you are staying somewhere with a mini kitchen, then go to a store and buy some Mucke's to cook. My husband used to purchase the packages of hot dogs, now that he's had a Mucke hot dog, he hasn't gone back to those "inferior" hot dogs. If you can't make your own, some of the hot dogs stand on the side of the road that you might see usually serve Mucke's.

When I go out for a hot dog, I go to Frankies in Brookfield. There are 6 other locations throughout the state if you aren't close to Brookfield. I've been going to Frankies for years, and now I get to take my son and pass on the tradition. My son likes to get the Dodger Dog and Jalapeno Poppers. Not adventurous to try a specialty dog? No problem, they also serve a plain hot dog for those who don't stray far from their ketchup and relish.

31. BEST INDIAN

After I had my son, my taste buds changed for the better. There were foods I didn't like before that I now really enjoyed. I liked Indian before, but now it is a favorite food of mine. Avon Indian Grill in Avon is the best place to get Indian. There are other Indian restaurants around, but I prefer the atmosphere at Avon Indian Grill. They are always pleasant and offer

39

suggestions when I want to be adventurous. The lunch buffet is a great way to try out new things on the menu. My favorite meal is samosa to start, chicken tikka masala, and Gulab Jamun for dessert. To drink, I get the mango lassi or a cocktail from the bar.

32. BEST ITALIAN

Italian is my husband's favorite food. When I took him to NYC for the first time, he really wanted to have Italian for dinner. I took him to my favorite restaurant in NYC, which is French. Needless to say, he still hasn't let me forget it. I have since made up for it with countless home-made dinners and date nights. Our favorite Italian spot is Paul's Pasta Shop in Groton. We love to sit outside and enjoy the view of the water. I love that they have "flavors of the week," which forces us to try new things, and they always become a new favorite. When they had the garlic herb pasta, my husband was in heaven. Sometimes, going with a classic is best, and they have the best fettuccini alfredo.

33. BEST FARMERS MARKET

Farmer's markets are an excellent way to support the local farmers. The Collinsville Farmers Market in Collinsville has multiple local vendors and live music every week. The market is once a week on Sunday, and it is a great way to support the community. There are shops and restaurants nearby; you can do your weekly shopping and stop at a restaurant for lunch after. I get my honey, salsa, and wine from their market.

34. BEST LOBSTER ROLL

One food that is very New England is the lobster roll. The Lobster Landing in Clinton has the best lobster rolls in all of New England. If you don't like lobster, they have you covered. They also have sausage, salad, and hot dogs. I love sitting outside with my lobster roll, New England clam chowder, and gelato on a clear summer day. In my opinion, there is nothing better than watching the sunset over the water after a good lobster roll.

35. BEST NEW ENGLAND CLAM CHOWDER

When I was growing up, an elderly neighbor couple adopted me as their surrogate granddaughter. I spent many summers with them in Niantic, going to the beach. My favorite part was stopping at Dad's Restaurant before heading home. To this day, my favorite thing to order is their New England clam chowder. Now, when I take my son to the beach, I carry on the tradition of stopping at Dad's Restaurant for the best clam chowder in New England.

36. BEST PIE

I am still mourning and processing the closure of The Pie Plate, which had the best pie in the state. Luckily I have other options to go to for my pie fix. A.C. Petersen Farms is a favorite of my family's to go and get pie. When in season, my favorite pie is the strawberry rhubarb a la mode. They have other delicious items on their menu, so be sure to save room for a slice of pie.

Hands down, a visit to the state wouldn't be complete without a visit to Lyman Orchards in Middlefield. They have a market where you can buy their award-winning pies or meals to go. They are all good, but you can never go wrong with a classic like an apple or pumpkin. There are plenty of activities for the family. You can pick your own strawberries, apples, and more. In the fall, they have events like their corn and sunflower mazes.

37. BEST PIZZA

Truth be told, I am not a pizza person. I am an extremist either preferring NY thin-crust or Sicilian thick. When it comes to 'za, my local favorite is E&D Pizza Company in Avon. The pizza shop opened in 2014 as a tribute to the owner's sons. I love taking my son there for our special mother/son date nights. He likes his pizza with pepperoni, onions, and garlic. We start off our meal with an order of wings, and sometimes garlic knots. The Caesar salad is so delicious; I am convinced it was crafted with help from the angels. When you start eating, place your order for the dessert pie since it takes 15 minutes to make. By the time you are done eating the meal, you can enjoy the addicting dessert pie made with Nutella, seasonal berries, and powdered sugar.

38. BEST PUB FOOD

My mom and I love pub food, and unique eateries, The Corner Pug in West Hartford, is both. I love all the different pictures of pugs that decorate the walls. The atmosphere is quirky and fun, with a full menu of all your pub favorites. The Shepherd's Pie and Yankee Pot Roast are my usual go-to's. For burger lovers, The Irish Nacho Burger has the perfect amount of heat. All of the dessert items are mouth-watering, but you have to try the apple pie tacos and the crème brulee.

39. BEST SUSHI

There are many options for sushi around the state; however, my favorite place to get sushi is Sakura Japanese Steak House. My best friend, Caroline, and I have been going there for many years. My favorite sushi rolls are the California roll, shrimp tempura, and cucumber roll. Caroline and I will also share sashimi in addition to our sushi rolls. For those who don't like sushi, Sakura also has wonderful hibachi dinners.

40. TACOS & TEQUILA

I love tacos and tequila. The best place for tacos and tequila is Ocho Café in West Hartford. My husband went for a date night recently and had a fabulous time. From the ambiance to the friendly waitstaff, we enjoyed ourselves immensely. Not only are their tacos the best, but they also make the best mole sauce. My favorite part was custom ordering a margarita. I got to pick the type of tequila from their list of over 60 varieties of tequila, mixer, and seasoning. For dessert, I strongly recommend the flan or tres leches cake.

41. BEST THAI

The award-winning Somewhere In Bangkok, located in Southington, is my favorite Thai restaurant.

The fruit smoothies or Thai ice tea are my drinks of choice. Their Bangkok egg roll, summer roll, and edamame are my go-to appetizers. Any of the stir-fried noodles or honey shrimp are my recommendations.

When I can't get to Southington, my other favorite Thai restaurant is The Elephant Trail in Avon. Their house salad comes with a Thai peanut dressing that is plate licking good. In the summer, I like to eat outside, looking out at the Farmington River. What sets The Elephant Trail apart from other restaurants in the area is that they offer a Thai cooking class. At the end of the class, you eat your dish with a paired wine and go home with a recipe card to make the dish again.

42. BEST WINGS

My son loves wings, and the spicier, the better. My son likes eating at J Timothy's Taverne because not only do they have some heat to them, the spiciness doesn't overshadow the flavor. The Food Network even said it was "… best buffalo sauce we've ever tasted!" I'm not surprised that the wings are award-winning; I was surprised to learn, however, that the "dirt" wing was invented at J Timothy's. Before you head back home, make sure to pick up a bottle of their award-winning buffalo sauce.

43. SWEET TOOTH

I want to shout out to several sweet tooth shops. In an environment that's cold more than it's hot, to make a famous year-round ice cream that's been around for a while is a feat. Yet J Foster Ice Cream does just that with their two stores in Avon and Simsbury. They create artisan ice cream with local dairy cows that are rBGH hormone-free, and only produce enough supply for a few days, ensuring freshness while supporting local farmers. My family's favorite flavors are cotton candy, mousse Trax, and girl scout choc indulge-mint.

When I go to Guilford, I have to stop by Hen & Heifer bakery. Every dessert is baked to French perfection. They have "basic" pastries like brownies and fruit tarts, sweet options, and savory options. My recommendation would be the Breton apple crumble or one of the cream puffs.

Dee's One Smart Cookie is the only non-GMO certified bakery in New England. It is gluten, dairy, and allergen bakery that raises the bar on all things sweet. The menu changes daily, so there is always something new to try and a new favorite to find. My husband's favorite dessert is cinnamon rolls, and when I know it is cinnamon roll day, I head over to get him some.

The Cake Gypsy has two locations, Avon and Granby. They sell cupcakes, cupcake kits, and cannolis. If a bakery has alternative options like gluten-free, those options are limited. Yet, Cake Gypsy is continuously updating its menu with gluten-free, vegan, and keto-friendly frosting & cakes. There are alternative treats such as edible cookie dough that doesn't spoil. Also, you'll find cakes, cakes made with cookie dough filling, and seasonal flavors such as Father's Day candied maple bourbon bacon cupcakes and donuts. For those with furbabies, there are pet-friendly cupcakes and treats. All baked flawlessly, moist, and tender without breaking apart after your first bite.

44. FOOD TOURS

Food tours are a great way to learn about the place you are visiting through the local restaurants. The Taste Of New Haven provides culinary walking tours with expert guides that will highlight the City of New Haven's culture and history. Currently, 9 tours offer a unique culinary experience that includes tapas, pizza, and the theater district. For the brave, there's a trick or eat spooky tour! My favorite tours are the taco, chocolate, and canal quarter tours. If you are looking for something specific, they have private tours with different cuisines and themes.

Another food tour I would recommend is Mystic Revealed. The topics, tour times, and restaurants highlighted are continually evolving, but the tour guides are always fun and knowledgeable. As a Melville fan, I still like learning about whaling, shipbuilding, and maritime history. The tour guides can recommend shops, hidden spots, and local color. I enjoy going on tours with other people. If you prefer a private tour, they can accommodate.

45. EAT WITH A VIEW

No matter the time of year, Connecticut is a beautiful state. I love that I can enjoy the mountains, valley, and ocean all within an hour's drive. Essex has The Essex Clipper Dinner Train. While you ride on a restored 1920's train, they serve a lovely 4-course meal. The rhythm of the ride is so relaxing, and the ambiance of the train makes the experience worth the trip. Another train ride activity I enjoy is the Chocolate & Wine train ride. While riding along, you get to sample pairings of fabulous wines and delectable chocolate. The murder mystery train is also entertaining!

The Essex Steam Train & Riverboat offers other activities if you don't want to do their dinner train. I like to ride on the train and riverboat excursions to see the scenery of Connecticut differently. Another exciting way to see Connecticut is to pedal a rail-bike. You get to see the stunning scenery along the Connecticut River.

For those with small children, they do a Day Out With Thomas. The characters from the beloved children show are at the station with activities and plenty of photo opportunities. There are also Family

Pirate Adventures, where you ride the train with a band of pirates.

There are many more to choose from; however, I would personally recommend the Tacos & Tequila Cruise on the riverboat.

46. FESTIVALS

Another reason why I love Connecticut in the fall is the festivals. Throughout the fall, there are many festivals, fairs, and carnivals to visit. Festivals are full of food, free samples, fun, and live music. If you've learned anything about me from this book, I think that it's a fact I love tacos. The taco festival is my favorite part of the year. What's not to like? You get to help decide on Connecticut's top taco! There is Lucha Libre Wrestling, a taco-eating contest, and a photo booth. Multiple food trucks and classic car festivals go on in different towns.

Bethlehem hosts the Connecticut Garlic & Harvest Festival. My husband and son love garlic, and they are in their element when we go. They visit and taste all the free samples of garlic around the festival. I love the live music, food choices, and vendor booths.

Southington has the Apple Harvest Festival. Like the other festivals, there are tons of food, crafts, and live music. I look forward to their apple fritters every year.

Old Saybrook hosts a chili festival in March. The best part, you get to vote and help decide the winner of the best chili.

47. FAIRS

Like the different themed festivals, there are many various fairs to go to from 4H to crafts. What is different about not only Connecticut but New England is that no one state has a state fair. Instead, all of New England comes together for The Big E, a six-state agricultural fair. For 17 days starting the second Friday after labor day, The Big E is the place to go. Conveniently located just over the border in Massachusetts, you need more than one day to truly experience everything The Big E has to offer. You could spend one day only at the Midway riding rides, a full day on food, and then another day just shopping.

The food! Every step you take, the diversity of smoked, fried, and baked goods fills the air, and your lungs, with scrumptious perfumes that will wet your tongue like raw honey.

A visit to the Avenue of States, you can visit all the state buildings for the individual New England states. Each building not only has things to see and buy, but you can also taste the local cuisines that make each state unique. Cranberries from Massachusetts, Maine baked potato, New Hampshire apple cider, and Vermont cheese, to name a few.

Every year, The Big E debuts a new signature food item. In 2009, they debuted the Craz-E Burger, a beef patty topped with bacon and nestled between a buttered and grilled Krispy Kreme glazed doughnut. I imagine as you read this, you are partly disgusted and partly curious. You will not regret it and will thank me for telling you about it. They are 1500 calories, and you will want more than one, so you may want to prepare for that with a 4k.

There is something for everyone in terms of entertainment and things to experience. There are two exhibition centers full of animals, a petting zoo, and parades. You can see craft winners, all the animals that win prizes, or just check out some Budweiser Clydesdales. There are three buildings full of crafts and vendors of all sorts. I love Egyptian culture. One year I purchased a beautiful perfume bottle from a vendor I cherish to this day. If that wasn't enough, The Big E has three stages for concerts.

48. SPECIAL OCCASIONS

To celebrate the divorce from my first marriage, my best friend Nick took me to Fleming's Prime Steakhouse & Wine Bar in West Hartford. Walking in to be seated was a luxurious experience. I was wearing a black cocktail dress, and the waiter offered me a black napkin instead of the usual white one. When we went, we planned just to snack on appetizers with some drinks. That night, they were offering an extraordinary three-course meal. I am so happy we decided to order it. The food was heavenly, absolute perfection, and hands down the best meal of my life. For starters, we had a Caesar salad that I still think about to this day. The fried capers and crispy prosciutto were a perfect complement to the salad. The filet mignon rested upon a pillow of garlic mashed potatoes.

Nick also took me to Cugino's Restaurant of Farmington for another special occasion. Cugino's was the first time I tried calamari, and the only place I will eat it. The chicken piccata with roasted potatoes were great compliments to the vintage wine selection they had available. Besides going there for dinner dates with friends, I've also been for meals after a funeral. The staff has always been attentive and lovely, especially when serving grieving families.

When I turned 21, my mother took me to Max a Mia in Avon for my first cocktail. I ordered a mouthwatering watermelon martini and delightful Chicken Parmigiano.

49. FOOD WITH A CONSCIOUS

There are several restaurants I like to support not only for their excellent food but because they are conscious of either allergens, GMO's, or worthy causes like my best steakhouse pick, Ted's Montana Grille, or even J Foster Ice Cream.

Bridgeport is the home of Bloodroot, which is a vegetarian feminist restaurant and bookstore. It started in the mid-1970s amongst other feminist businesses. Specializing in ethnic vegan and vegetarian cuisine, Bloodroot is the type of business we need to support.

One of my go-to lunch places is The Sweet Beet in Granby. Everything they serve is vegan and free of gluten, soy, peanuts, and GMOs. They are supporters of local farms and small businesses, which I love about them. The soup of the day is always good, and the curry chickpea sandwich is addicting. They have grab n' go eats, sweets, and enticing drinks.

In New Preston is The White Horse Country Pub & Restaurant. The restaurant offers a separate menu for vegan, gluten-free, and vegetarian Plow to Plate items. The Plow to Plate program advocates healthy good, promoting local agricultural economy and disease prevention.

50. MUSIC & ART SCENE

I have been going to Lasalle Market & Deli in Collinsville my entire life. My parents would stop at Lasalle's for a treat every week. I love that Lasalle supports the local artist with their Market Gallery. Lasalle does not profit from the sale of the artwork, and 20% is donated to substance abuse programs. On Friday's they have their Friday Night Open Mic. I have gone several times, and it is fun! You get to meet different people, listen to good music, and eat good food.

Lucky Lou's in Wethersfield is another fun place to eat and enjoy live music. There are generous gluten-free options like the Rosemary Chicken Lollipops. I enjoy ordering the super chili nachos, Knob Creek Bourbon straight, and relax to the music.

BONUS TIP 1: HORROR FANS

My good friend Evan is a huge fan of all things horror. In Connecticut, we have tons of sights to see if you are like Evan and love horror.

Located in New Haven, Church-on-the-green has a crypt of 137 graves. These graves hold New England's earliest residents. The members of the church are friendly and knowledgeable, and that's why I recommend doing one of the free tours of the crypt. Also in New Haven is the grave of the New Haven urban legend, Midnight Mary.

Bristol is home to Witch's Dungeon, a seasonal movie monster museum. Witch's Dungeon is the longest-running classic horror movie attraction in the country. The museum runs on weekends from September and October.

If vampires are your thing, you may have heard about the Jewett City Vampires. Griswold has the graves of the Ray family thought to be plagued by a vampire.

For those familiar with the book and film of the same name, *The Haunting in Connecticut,* you can see the "possessed" house that inspired the book and movie in Southington.

For the serial killer fans, you can take a trip to Windsor. Windsor has the home of a famous female serial killer. Her story inspired the Broadway hit "Arsenic and Old Lace." Be warned; the house is a private residence. You may take pictures but be respectable.

My friend Evan is a huge fan of *Friday the 13th*; if visiting, you can meander through Washington, New Preston, and Kent to see where the film was made.

BONUS TIP 2: IT'S ABANDONED

To see how nature takes over once humans are no longer involved can be done by visiting Gay City State Park in Hebron. You can walk around the ruins of the abandoned 18-century town. Some of the ruins can be seen from the hiking trails. I like to go into the woods, off the path to discovering different parts of the town. Be warned; if you plan on camping, you do need a permit. There is a cemetery for ghost hunters. The town has been taken over by nature, but you can still see what remains.

Driving down I-84 at night in Waterbury, you may see a cross lit up on top of a hill. That cross is part of the abandoned religious-themed amusement park,

Holy Land USA. In the daytime, you can explore the abandoned park.

In Hartford, there is a steel and chrome diner from the 1940s named the Comet. It is a weird and exciting feeling to see something frozen in time.

Newton has an abandoned psychiatric hospital, Fairfield Hills Hospital. At one time, the hospital housed more than 4,000 patients. Since 2015 the town has been doing renovations around the grounds. Sadly, the underground tunnels have been removed or filled with concrete.

In Waterford, by the water, is the Seaside Sanatorium. Interestingly, the brick building was America's first medical facility designed to offer heliotropic treatment. The treatment was for children with tuberculosis.

Farmington has an abandoned depression-era zoo. The Shade Swamp Sanctuary is hidden just off the highway. Putting in Shade Swamp to your GPS is the best way to navigate getting there.

BONUS TIP 3: AS SEEN ON TV

There has been an increase of television shows being filmed in Connecticut thanks to the production tax credit. One production that has always called Connecticut home is The WWE in Stamford.

When I was a teenager, I was obsessed with the show "Gilmore Girls." Stars Hollow doesn't exist, but you can visit the places that inspired the television show. Washington, New Milford, Bantam, and Litchfield are among the towns to visit to get the "Gilmore Girls" experience.

Washington is home to the Mayflower Inn; you may know it better as the Independence Inn. In Washington is Marty's Café (Luke's Diner), The Washington Food Market (Doose's Market), and The Hickory Stick Bookshop (Stars Hollow Books). New Milford's town green has a gazebo that should look familiar to "Gilmore Girls" fans. Be sure to check your calendars and come during the Gilmore Girls Fan Fest!

BONUS TIP 4: UNIQUE MUSEUMS

Museum of Natural And Other Curiosities – Hartford

P.T. Barnum Museum – Bridgeport

New England Carousel Museum – Bristol

American Clock and Watch Museum – Bristol

Vintage Radio and Communications Museum –
   Windsor

Danbury Railway Museum – Danbury

Barker Character, Comic, and Cartoon Museum –
   Cheshire

American Museum of Tort Law – Winchester

Connecticut Air and Space Center – Stratford

Haddam Shad Museum – Haddam

Ballard Institute and Museum of Puppetry – Storrs

Timexpo Museum – Waterbury

Dinosaurs

Dinosaur State Park – Rocky Hill

Powder Hill Dinosaur Park – Middlefield

The Dinosaur Place – Oakdale

For the Kids

Supercharged – Montville

IT Adventure Ropes Course – New Haven

Lake Compounce Theme Park – Bristol

Urban Air Adventure Park – Orange

Nomads Adventure Quest – South Windsor

International Skating Center of Connecticut –
   Simsbury

The Great Outdoors

Brownstone Exploration & Discovery Park – Portland

Farmington River Tubing – New Hartford

Hike the Heublein Tower in Simsbury. Check out the two exciting events per year, Hike To The Mic and Tower Toot.

The waterfall in the Campbell Falls State Park Reserve – Norfolk

Canoe or Kayak with Huck Finn Adventures – Avon

The Cove – Old Wethersfield

Orchards – Glastonbury

Elizabeth Park – Hartford

Silver Sands State Park – Milford

The Observatory at the Westport Astronomical Society – Westport

Sleeping Giant State Park - Hamden

Rocky Neck State Park – East Lyme

Visit one of the oldest trees in New England, Dewey-Granby Oak – Granby

Visit the largest tree in Connecticut, The Pinchot Sycamore. – Simsbury

People's State Forest – Barkhamsted

BONUS TIP 5: UNIQUE THINGS TO SEE

Charles Island, the "cursed" island that is allegedly home to Captain Kidd's lost treasure. – Milford

Hospital Rock, the carved patient list, is all that remains of the Todd-Wadsworth Smallpox Hospital. – Farmington

Judges Cave, where Edward Whalley, William Goffe, and John Dixwell hid after sentencing King Charles I to death. – New Haven

Ancient Burying Ground – Hartford

Site of the first public payphone – Hartford

Hartford circus fire memorial – Hartford

Flood of 1936 Marker – Hartford

South Slope of Mount Frissell is where the highest point in Connecticut was incorrectly memorialized. – Salisbury

Talcott Basalt Lava Pillows – Meriden

BONUS TIP 6: FUN FACTS

The state insect is the Praying Mantis.

The state animal is the Sperm Whale.

The state song is "Yankee Doodle."

The state flower is the Mountain-laurel.

The state bird is the American Robin.

The state mineral is Garnet.

The state tree is the Charter (white) Oak.

The New Haven District Telephone Company published the first telephone book in February 1878. The telephone book contained only 50 names.

Connecticut is home to the oldest continuously published newspaper, The Hartford Courant. The Hartford Courant has been publishing papers since 1764.

In addition to the first hamburger, Connecticut is home to the first Polaroid camera, helicopter, and color television.

The first US automobile law was passed in 1901 in my state. The speeds were limited to 12 miles per hour in cities and 15 on country roads. The Ford T top speeds could reach 40-45 miles per hour.

OTHER RESOURCES

https://www.ctvisit.com/

https://portal.ct.gov/About/State-Symbols

https://portal.ct.gov/DEEP/State-Parks/Trail-and-Camping-Maps---CT-State-Parks-and-Forests

https://www.thebige.com/

https://www.atlasobscura.com/things-to-do/connecticut/

https://www.gilmoregirlsfanfest.com/

READ OTHER BOOKS BY CZYK PUBLISHING

Greater Than a Tourist- St. Croix US Birgin Islands USA: 50 Travel Tips from a Local by Tracy Birdsall

Greater Than a Tourist- Toulouse France: 50 Travel Tips from a Local by Alix Barnaud

Children's Book: *Charlie the Cavalier Travels the World* by Lisa Rusczyk

Eat Like a Local

Follow *Eat Like a Local on* Amazon.
Join our mailing list for new books
http://bit.ly/EatLikeaLocalbooks

Made in the USA
Middletown, DE
31 July 2020